For all the children who miss someone special - may these pages make you feel seen, supported and never alone. To my parents, who first shared with me the quiet magic of snow and its gentle reminders of love - your stories became the heart of this one.

This paperback edition first published in 2025 by Padgett Publishing.

First edition, 2025.

British Library Cataloguing in Publication Data available.

ISBN: 978-1-0369-2791-2

What the Snow Brings

by Emily Padgett

Emily loved the snow. Every winter, when the first snowflakes began to fall, she would rush outside to catch them on her tongue. She loved how each snowflake was unique, no two were ever the same.

But this year, the snow felt different. It was the first time Emily would see the snow without her dad beside her. Emily missed him more than she could put into words. Everything felt quieter, and the world seemed a little colder.

One afternoon, Emily stood by the window, watching the snow fall gently outside. She wished more than anything that her dad could be there with her, enjoying the snow like they used to.

Then, Emily remembered something her dad had always told her when she was younger: 'Whenever you see the snow, think of it as a gift from those we loved. The snowflakes fall from the sky, reminding us of all the love that's still with us, even when someone isn't around.'

Emily stood still, watching the snowflakes float gently to the ground.

She closed her eyes for a moment, and imagined her dad smiling down at her, sending each snowflake as a reminder of the love he had for her.

Now, every time Emily saw the snow falling, she would remember her dad's words. Each snowflake was a reminder of the love that never leaves, even when the person who gave it isn't there.

Emily realised that as long as the snow fell, her dad's love would always be there, just like the snowflakes - gentle, constant and full of love.

Isabella loved to look at the stars, but the one thing that always caught her eye was the moon.

Her grandad had once told her that there was a man on the moon who watched over everyone, especially during the night. But what made the moon even more special was the story her grandad used to tell her. He'd say, 'I hold up a giant torch to the sky and shine it on the moon, so everyone can see it glow.'

This year, as Isabella looked up at the moon, it felt different. Isabella missed her grandad more than ever. She missed his laughter, the way he used to tell her stories and how his voice always made her feel safe.

But then, as she stared at the moon's soft light, Isabella remembered what her grandad had always said: 'I'm the man who lights the moon, shining my torch for you, so you'll always know I'm here.'

Isabella smiled a little. She imagined her grandad, holding his torch high, lighting up the night sky just like he used to say.

Even though he wasn't with her anymore, she felt that his love still shone down on her, as bright as the moon itself. It was his way of reminding her that no matter what, she was never alone.

Now, every time Isabella looks up at the moon, she remembers her grandad and the special way he used to light up the sky. The moon's bright, comforting glow is his way of telling her that his love is still shining down on her, just like the torch he held to make the moon so bright at night.

Alfie loved spending time outside, especially on quiet mornings when the world felt still and peaceful. One morning, as he played in the garden, he noticed something unusual: a soft, white feather lying on the ground.

It was perfectly clean, light and delicate, as if it had been placed there just for him. Alfie remembered something his mum had told him once. She had said that sometimes, when we feel lonely or miss someone, feathers appear as little signs of love from the people we care about.

They might come from the sky, floating gently down to remind us that our loved ones are always near, watching over us, even when we can't see them. Alfie thought about all the people who share their love with him - his mum and dad, his grandparents, his best friends, even his dog!

They were the ones he loved the most. With the feather in his hand, he could feel their constant love - comforting and soft, just like the feather itself.

Alfie smiled and imagined that it had floated down from the sky. It wasn't just any feather - it was a sign that even though one day someone he loved so dearly might not be there, their love would still be all around him.

From that day on, whenever Alfie found a feather - whether it was white, brown, or any colour - he would stop and remember that it was a special gift reminding him of a loved one.

He knew that the feathers weren't just tiny pieces of nature; they were little symbols of love, floating down from the sky to remind him that those he cared about were always nearby, in his heart and watching over him with love.

Emma and Riley were not only brother and sister, they were best friends who loved doing everything together. On rainy days, when the sun began to peek through the clouds, they would run outside, eager to see if they could spot a rainbow. They believed rainbows were a little bit of magic in the sky, a sign that something beautiful was coming after the rain.

Their nanna used to tell them a special story about rainbows. She said that every rainbow was a gift she ordered from the Rainbow Man, who lived in the clouds. 'I ask him to send a rainbow so you know I love you, and I'm always thinking of you.' It made each rainbow feel even more special.

One afternoon, after a summer storm, Emma and Riley rushed outside, looking up at the sky. Sure enough, a bright rainbow appeared, stretching across the sky in a perfect arc of colours. The rain had just stopped, and the world felt fresh and new. They remembered how Nanna would always smile and tell them the rainbow was a little message from her, just to remind them of her love.

As they stood together, watching the colours shimmer in the sky, Emma smiled a little as she knew the rainbow was a gift of love, just for them. She knew her nanna would be talking to the Rainbow Man, asking him to send them a rainbow, just like she used to.

In that moment, Emma felt like Nanna's love would always shine down on them through every colour of the rainbow. It was as if the rainbow itself was a hug from her, a reminder that love never really goes away. It stays with us, in the memories, in the moments we share, and even in the rainbows that appear after the storm.

From that day on, whenever Emma and Riley saw a rainbow, they remembered their nanna's story. The rainbow became their special sign - a reminder that love, no matter where it comes from, will always shine through, just like the bright colours of a rainbow after the rain.

Summer was sitting quietly in the garden one afternoon, feeling a little lonely. She missed someone she loved, someone who was no longer with her. It didn't matter who it was - it could be a family member, a friend, or even a pet. Sometimes, the sadness would sneak up on her and she would find herself wishing they were still there, laughing and spending time with her.

As Summer sat there, lost in her thoughts, she suddenly heard the cheerful, familiar song of a robin coming from the tree above. She looked up and saw the bright red chest of the robin as it hopped from branch to branch, its little wings fluttering in the breeze. Summer smiled, feeling a little lighter.

She had always heard that robins were special. They were often thought to be messengers from loved ones who were no longer with us. Whenever a robin appeared, it was a sign that someone who loved her was thinking of her, sending a little message from the sky.

Summer closed her eyes for a moment and whispered, 'I know you're here with me.' It didn't matter who the robin was from - it was enough to know that the love of someone she missed was still with her, in the gentle flutter of the robin's wings and the sweetness of its song.

From that day on, whenever Summer saw a robin, she remembered that love never truly goes away. Whether it is a family member, a friend, or even a beloved pet, the robin is a reminder that those we love are always near, sending us messages of love and comfort in the most unexpected ways.

Brodie loved watching the sunsets, especially when the sky turned pink and gold. It made him feel peaceful and calm, as if the world was giving him a big hug at the end of the day. He would sit on the hill and watch the colours change, and for a moment, everything seemed right.

One evening, as Brodie watched the sunset, he remembered something his mum had once told him: 'The sunsets remind us that even when things feel tough or sad, the world keeps going, and tomorrow is always a new day.'

Brodie smiled, thinking about how the sunset marked the end of one day and the promise of another. He knew that no matter what had happened during the day, the sun would rise again, bringing with it the chance for a fresh start, and a new beginning.

The next morning, Brodie woke up early to see the sunrise. As the first light peeked over the horizon, he felt hopeful. The sky turned soft shades of pink and orange, and the sunlight filled the world with warmth and light. It reminded him that every day is a new opportunity to smile, try again and appreciate the love and kindness around him.

Now, every sunset and sunrise reminds Brodie that no matter what happens, the world keeps turning. There are good days and hard days, but the sun will always rise again, bringing with it a new day full of chances, new memories and love.

A Note from the Author

I'm a mum of two, a qualified early years teacher and the manager of an early years setting. With a BA in Primary and Early Years Teaching and a Masters in Education, I've spent my life dedicated to nurturing children in their most formative years. Early childhood is a precious time - one that I believe should be filled with love, understanding and support, especially when children are faced with difficult emotions like grief.

This book is more than just a story. It is a personal journey. It was created from my own experience of loss, shaped by the lessons I learned through childhood and the quiet wisdom passed down by my parents. Growing up, I was introduced to the comforting belief in snow as a symbol of remembering those we've lost. That idea stayed with me - helping me feel connected to my loved ones, even in their absence. It offered a sense of peace that gently carried me through my own grief.

My background in education and my work with young children has shown me just how important it is to support little ones as they make sense of complex emotions. Grief, even for the youngest child, is real and powerful - and so is their capacity for love, healing and hope when we guide them with care.

Through this book, I hope to offer a light - a way for children to see that even in the darkest moments, love doesn't leave us. It surrounds us. It stays with us. All I want is to help every child feel seen, supported and reminded that the people we love are always with us in some way.

This story is part of my heart. It's helped me grow and heal and I hope it will do the same for you and the little ones you share it with.

Emily x

Printed in Dunstable, United Kingdom

65782481R00020